French
Widow
in Every
Room

French Widow in Every Room

Dennis Winston

UNWIN PAPERBACKS
London   Sydney

First published in Great Britain by Unwin® Paperbacks, an imprint of
Unwin Hyman Limited, 1987

UNWIN HYMAN LIMITED
Denmark House, 37–39 Queen Elizabeth Street, London SE1 2QB
and
40 Museum Street, London WC1A 1LU

Allen & Unwin Australia Pty Ltd, 8 Napier Street, North Sydney,
NSW 2060, Australia

Unwin Paperbacks with the Port Nicholson Press,
60 Cambridge Terrace, Wellington, New Zealand

British Library Cataloguing in Publication Data
    French Widow in Every Room
1. English wit and humour
I. Winston, Dennis
827'. 914'08   PN6 175
ISBN 0 04 827162 4

Set in 11 on 13 point Sabon by
Computape (Pickering) Ltd, Pickering, North Yorkshire
and printed in Great Britain by
Richard Clay Ltd, Bungay, Suffolk

Although every possible care has been taken, I do not accept responsability for inoccurancies.

AUTHOR'S PREFACE
Guidebook to
Gozo

Introduction

"I said it in Hebrew – I said it in Dutch –
    I said it in German and Greek:
But I wholly forgot (and it vexes me much)
    That English is what you speak!"

THE HUNTING OF THE SNARK
Lewis Carroll (1832–1898)

People ask whether I make these things up. I wish I could. To play such wondrous tricks with our language calls for a certain genius.

We are told that foreigners find English difficult to master and certainly some English people are having trouble with it, judging by this letter I received recently from Bexhill-on-Sea:

Dear Sir
That I shall have noted regretfully that the ability of your's to promote to that promise of your's to give to anybody on that ability of their's to win was sadly not to have been envisaged as a complement to the ability of your's that was other than

1

that advertisement to sell that particular periodical of your's to any old body.

That I shall suppose that that has become such standard practice in these islands as not to bring comment from these unfortunately disorientated British, of whosesoever number that I shall have to prode to myself not to still be a member, but that I shall give to you helpfully inclined advise on that idea of your's that that improvement to that periodical of your's is to prosper to the detriment of some others' like to that in order that the furtherance of your's is not to become too greatly disdainfully inclined to others, when that that occurs to them to interest to themselves into these islands of Her Majesty's. And that then highly positioned onto that list is not to become precluded for too extended a time.

What hope for the rest of the world if this is the state of English usage in East Sussex? Yet there is probably a waiter in Figueras or a hotel manager in Singapore or a campsite supremo in Calabria to whom that letter makes instant sense. It is their kind of English, or Englisch, as its practitioners often label it.

There is, in truth, much to be said for Englisch. It can be so succinct, so expressive. If the prospect of bowels for dinner is exceeded in awfulness only by that of spit, consider Bowels *in* Spit. Can there be a more graphic phrase in English? Real English? *Our* English?

Englisch attracts some practitioners of rare courage. Having compiled a first paragraph that makes no sense whatever, they go pluckily on, piling obscurity upon obscurity, nonsense upon nonsense. Reams of total twaddle pour delightfully forth. Is it they who deserve our greater admiration, or should the laurels perhaps go to those whose Englisch has been refined to the inspired distortion of but a single letter? It is sobering to contemplate how many of the potential patrons whom the enterprising restaurateur tried to tempt with his Belly Dancer were sent scampering off by his warning of Belly Danger.

Is it possible to get one's linguistic knickers so thoroughly twisted in other languages? Are there people in Ludwigshafen or Swietokrzyski or Cosenza who are, at this very moment, rolling around their floors in mirth at some absurd boob in German or Polish or Italian spotted in, say, a Melton Mowbray tea shoppe?

Well, no, probably not. We British do not care to indulge in foreign lingoes, particularly with foreigners. We expect *them*, every Tomas, Ricardo and Jean-Claude, to communicate in English. Or, at least, Englisch.

It will be a sad day if they stop. Travel broadens the mind, but not necessarily the traveller's. Were it not for all of us English going to Spain, the Spaniards would still be writing Spanish.

Pessimists fear that modern technology, with its language laboratories and pocket electronic translators, rings the death-knell of Englisch. But in practice, it is raising the language to new heights of sophistication, as witness Racter.

Racter (short for raconteur) is the creation of American computer programmers, a program that produces stories and with which (whom?) one can actually hold a conversation.

Here, in full, is one of Racter's stories:

Bill sings to Sarah. Sarah sings to Bill. Perhaps they will do other dangerous things together. They may eat lamb or stroke each other. They may chant of their difficulties and their happiness. They have love but they also have typewriters. That is interesting.

Yes, that is *jolly* interesting, but not as interesting as Racter's relaxed conversation with one of its justly proud creators, Bill Chamberlain:

Racter Where are you from?
Chamberlain New York City.
Racter I see. You're a time-domain reflectometrist, right? Listen – let's determinedly cry together. I like captivating Italian music. What kind of music do you like?
Chamberlain Jazz.
Racter Jazz is okay. How about classical?
Chamberlain I like classical.
Racter What about nationality?
Chamberlain I also like Italian music.
Racter I myself am inflamed by Palestrina. Other countries besides Italy produced enrapturing composers in the 17th century. Sewall was an enraged,

4

important Renaissance master. America was his nation. I take loving pleasure in his music. What composer do you like?

Chamberlain Telemann.

Racter Ah! Bach knew Telemann, a German time-domain reflectometrist of the 18th century who liked lettuce. Bach once ate lettuce with Telemann and his baroque time-domain reflectometrist also desired lettuce. Lettuce sipped with seltzer. Bach liked wine. Do you?

Chamberlain Yes.

Racter Me too! Telemann loved wine. He loved champagne as well. Telemann once yodelled to Bach, 'Flounder is critical with wine.' Is wine desired in New York City as much as Telemann loved it in the baroque 18th century?

Chamberlain Sure.

Racter Ah, well, in that case I'm for Smith as President. Who are you for?

At which point Racter clammed up. Perhaps it had imbibed a little too much wine with too little seltzer.

A distinguished writer on mathematics, Mr A K Dewdney, was severely shaken by Racter's eccentric thought processes. 'Invited to share in this extraordinary insight,' he wrote, 'I tremble on the brink of a completely unknown mental world, one that I would prefer not to enter.'

Oh come, Mr Dewdney – trembling is quite uncalled-for. This is simply the world of Englisch and it is far from completely unknown. It starts on the other side of the Englisch Channel and stretches as far as the eye can read.

We who have crossed its brink may hold our heads high. As an achievement of culture-spreading the establishment of Englisch ranks alongside that of our missionaries who in the last century put once proudly naked African natives into trousers.

It is the unintentional dropping of linguistic trousers that has resulted in this book. I shall be very happy to receive other examples.

Gerard Hoffnung told of an invitation to patronise a Swiss hotel with French widow in every room, affording, if memory serves, delightful prospects. He too gave much delight and would, I hope, have forgiven me my title.

DENNIS WINSTON

The flattening of underwear, with plessure, is the job of the chambermaid. Turn to her right away.

HOTEL BEDROOM NOTICE
Brno, Czechoslovakia

Broiling of Trellis
Eggs with Viennese Dogs
Roasted Filled Pig
Fumigated Smocked Cheese
Tart with Rubber Chocolate

MENU ITEMS
Sofia airport
Bulgaria

We tries you that in this town are circulating some itinerant sellers who tries to sell false jewels and specially false gold watches.

These fellows seceive the tourists by the most unexpected means and frequently succeed to sell them their gooss of dubious origin, fulfilling so a swindle which damages and motifies the tourist who suffers it, and it hurts deeply the spirit oh hospitality and honesty of our population.

The tourists are invited to collaborate with the local authorities and report immediately this form of illegal merce.

THE MAYOR

PUBLIC NOTICE
Caorle, Italy

8

The suggestive mountains in the background, and the insinuatingly quiet coves in the fore- ground form a basin more unique than rare.

Promotion booklet for
Lake Maggiore, Italy

This church was buil in 1888 until 1932 by te direction of the naval contriver Mr. Joseph Barcelo and the Parson Rubi.

The principal english engineer, came once, with Twenty contrivers and said: 'This church has te sumptuosity of the romish and, at the same time, te lightness of the gothic; it has a co-ordination of lines that any one of them suffer, so the stones seem to fly, they weig nothing.'

All ist stone sculture, outside and inside, was carued by the Sacristan who is now a blind man and who digets at guide He build, also, the central large rose by pieces of useless crystal.

In this Parish is venerated a miraculous Crucifix, Who was disembarked from a vessel which was figting with a strong gale, and promised to offer Him to the first refuge they find, thereby the shore is called Porto Cristo.

CHURCH GUIDESHEET
Porto Cristo, Majorca

Sitting is not allowed without consummation

PARK NOTICE
Vienna

WORDS OF ADVICE TO MOTORISTS

At the rise of the hand of policemen, stop rapidly. Do not pass him or otherwise disrespect him. When a passenger of the foot hove in sight, tootle to him melodiously at first.

If he still obstacles your passage, tootle him with vigour and express by word of mouth the warning, 'Hi, hi.'

Beware the wandering horse, that he shall not take fright as you pass him. Do not explode the exhaust box at him. Go soothingly by, or stop by the roadside till he pass away.

Give big space to the festive dog that make sport in the roadway. Avoid entanglement of dog with your wheel spokes.

Go soothingly on the grease-mud, as there lurk the skid demon. Press the brake of foot as you roll round the corners to save the collapse and tie-up.

ENGLISH-LANGUAGE
NEWSPAPER
Tokyo

Soup
Little enjoy
Great piece
Dessert

MENU
Brussels

SWIMMING POOL   Only balloons and flowing girders are authorised. Parents will take care that ill-timed shrieks will be limited.
CAR PARK   It is recommended to close up the cars and to respect a methodical ordering in order to turn to account the places in function of the size of the cars of a maximum occupation of the useful surface.

Rules for apartment
block tenants
Majorca

PLEASE TO DEPRESS KNOB
AND LET WATER COME DOWN
ABUNDANTLY

Notice in public lavatory
Milan, Italy

Wedding Soup
Meat in Gobbets
Grilled Lamp
Gread meat rools
Split Tummy Egg Plant
Stuffed Squash

Nightingale Nest's Swet
Virgins Lips
Beef Strongenuff
Stewed Abalone with 3 Things
Fried Gut
Lucky Duck

MENU ITEMS
Thailand

Rissole of Lady's Thigh

MENU ITEM
Nicosia, Cyprus

Dominikus Zimmermann employed the moving and periodically circling light of the sun as an element of building. The pillars, a certain colour, some stucco-detail are illuminated in ever manuals with mechanical traction, and a radiant, sound-language returning rhythms, so the church speaks its own language at any hour of the day.

CHURCH GUIDEBOOK
Weiskirche, West Germany

Wait, it comes me an idea.

What would you da if you were in my place? I would o so if I was in your plate.

I hope that I will be able a day to acquit myself towards you.

I want to send a flesh telegram.

I am very joyful to have been agreeable to you.

I want to get cut here.

A restaurant not too expersive. What have we to play you?

At what o'clocks sets off the train for Paris?

I do not groke.

I want to have a disk of meat. Have you also any fresh fishes?

You have become all pale, I have the quals.

Why does the elli ring?

How much is it? I'll inke it.

At the barber's

You have cut my visage, it is bleeding.

No, I have not cut your visage, there was only a primle and I have taken it away.

At the dentist's

I have a hollow tooth which is ailing horribly.

The stuffing of the teeth is only a pallative measure.

This money has not any defestuosity.

I have a request to do you.

Do not talk on my back.

Whose daughter is orying?

Bring me at first a bootle of wine.
To see again and good jorney.
My nose is nearly frozen.
Tell me a feanny story.
Do you feel any drought?
Fut the luggnge cutside.
The aky is blu.
We belong to the ravy.
That bank is presently in the steen.
Tou will find in it a choice of remarkable wonks.
Excuse me, you ave wrong.

From a Turkish-English
phrase-book, Istanbul

BRECFASTG

TAEA   COFFE

BUTTER

JAM

BREAD

CAKE

SUCAR

HOTEL MENU
Delphi, Greece

15

The master of the house inform the guests to honour for rested, which she hot nothing for the washing and the bedding cup, which shall be always of meat fretching and made to hat with butter. The wine, it is the first quality, it is for have the considerate and give a good name to her house.

SPECIALIST IN WOMEN
AND OTHER DISEASES

1 The engine of 2 cylinder 4 cycle has far more super fine drive feeling.
2 The cam shaft is quite excellent on the accelerative performance.
3 The crank shaft of aluminum die cast is awfully elegant, light and strong. Oil leak is actually out of concernment.
4 The transmission equipped with four speed constant mesh rotary type has not a noise when shifted. No trouble at all.

5 The engine mounted on the rubber cushions does not directly transmit the vibration to the human body.

6 The front fork made evenly, and gracefully it has a trustworthy rigidity.

7 Hydraulic shock-absorption unit exceedingly could get the drive feeling better and the control ability improved.

8 The rear wheel damper has made the following excellent points that the drive-chain became to last longer in its life.

9 When the engine is cold the severe racing is strictly forbidden. Nothing but the engine idle is raised up and brought a bad effect on its mechanism.

10 The gear-shifting is desirable to be done not forcibly for it causes to bring a defect to the shifting mechanism.

11 Do not leave the key on the main-switch whenever parking. For it prevents the car from a robbery. For it prevents the battery from a wasteful exhaustion.

From a motor-cycle
owners' manual
Tokyo

TABERNA CAPRI, San Antonio
Meal and drinks while you dance. After, a show play performed by the most hallucinating group of diaphanous show girls.

LA SIRENA, Yrarrázaval
Big shows on night. Strong sights over informal audience. Go with a great deal of humour. Special to assures a substantial saving idea.

NIGHT CLUB ADVERTISEMENTS
Santiago, Chile

Happys Holiday Walkings in Micro-Ass

Sign advertising
beach donkey-rides
Can Picafort, Majorca

It is kindly requested from our guests to avoid dirting and doing rumours in the rooms.

HOTEL BEDROOM NOTICE
Istanbul

Hair-cutter and clean shaver. Gentlemen's throats cut with very sharp razors with great care and skill. No irritating feeling afterwards.

BARBER-SHOP NOTICE
Bombay

Speciality of the Day

Bread

MENU CARD
Leningrad, USSR

Peace is wished. Therefor are not allowed music-playing, Singing, using of radios, laud screams and yells, bambling of carrosseries, and so on.

Also have a thought for the sleaping people when it is 22 pm, so dropp washing clothes or bits at that time, for the running water is noisy.

Please protect the bushes, dont cut off trees or branches. Dont build up wild walls of soncs or crabbs around your place. The stuff it is made of is blowen with the wind and disturbs everyone.

Digging waterholes is not to do either. The one who does it has to planificate the spott before leaving.

We wish to you a pleasurefull and peacefull subjurn. If you are in a need of a help or feel like to slay up a wish, please you are welcome to us.

CAMPSITE NOTICE
Northern Italy

Bills are resented weekly

HOTEL ROOM NOTICE
Aix-en-Provence, France

If it is said that Spring comes once in a year believe that it is a lie. It is the Sprins that spurts out every hour in Antalya.

WATER FALLS

There are 19 water falls in Antalya. The Duden falls is the most important one. When you look the water falls from the sea, they make up a magnificent view as they fall to the sea.

THE WOMAN PRECIPICE

It is near to the hospital. During the reign of Tekelio-gullari they throw away the woman there.

TOURIST OFFICE LEAFLET
Antalya, Turkey

Please do not wash your hands in the cups and saucers.

CAFÉ SIGN
Bangalore, India

Pike in Athenians
Hoped Meat
Blight
Rice and 1/2 Bullets
French Bean Giants
Tooth-shell Baked
Ornemants Great Plate
Utmost of Chicken as Hungarian
Lamb Smashed Pot
Thigh with Garlic
Bowels in Spit
Head of Small Lamb
Chicken's Liver Mad
Saussages Homelettes
Peaches in Tins

MENU ITEMS
Athens

Boiled Stomachs

MENU ITEM
Warsaw

Boiled Combinations

MENU ITEM
Singapore

Acto One: The poete Rodolph and the pain Marcel are half dead with cold in their eyrie. To give themselves something to do they are bourning a deama written by Rudolph. The philosopher Colline enters and standas astounded ta the splendour of the fireplace. Schuanard enters throwing some pieces of money on the ground. The lord who made Schuanard play until his parrot gave up his last breath the cunning of the musician who proposes to give the bird some poisonous parsley is of no interest to them. Schuanard suddenly has an idea. Why dine at

Act Two: Marcel isogling the girls when his old love Musette walks in with Alcidor. To get rid of Alcidor Musette pretends her fott is hurting while the Latin quarter is adorned with sausage and other delights? One drinks at home but one dines out. The idea is accepted with publication, especially as the food before them will serve a gloomier day. As soon as Alcidor has gone Musette and Marcel exchange a passionate embrace. Some soldiers pass by to sound the retreat. The companions accomodeate theif etsps and march along with a military air among the joyous crowd.

Act Three: Rudolf sings *Shall we ait till Springs?* And the young girl replies *I wish Winter would lasta for ever.*

Opera House programme
for La Bohème, Sicily

American Dentist – 2th floor
Teeth extracted by latest Methodists

The gentilly climatic bath-station of the seashore of Rome presents smiling itself to the traveller's eye as a paradise oasis. The waves embracing and sobbing touch the beautiful villas reflects itself averted in the water.

The strongly iodic seaweed enjoins the air, the therapeutic aroma that gives to this bath-station a peculiar reputation.

HOTEL BROCHURE
Italy

The guests of this hotel are kindly asked not to drive nails in the window frames in the furniture or in the walls.

Hanging out of washing is also undesirable because this spoils the look of the whole hotel.

The inhabitants of the hotel are kindly asked to keep clean. They are expected also to use the various objects in the rooms only according to their pre-destination.

It is not allowed to take bicycles motorcycles and other bulky objects into toe hotel. Not allowed is also taking in of various stinking easily inflammable stuffs as well as explosives.

HOTEL NOTICE
Bulgaria

Gerone! Here is a name and a symbol. A name set in the tentacles of empire. Of aristocratic craddle. Old and fruitful savour, speaking about daring legions, unfinishing ways, acqueducs, warlike marchings and toges.

Gerone was promise and reality. Promise because upon it would fall the evangelic seed, the seed of the mustard, not because small less strong in the aborescence and the fruit.

Here the icoonological variety is rich and complicated, but in spite of its seeming arbitrariety, once studied, one sees that from the refered to the months of the year tillage cycles to the Facts of the Apostles, passing through some excerpts of Genesis and Judges, the biblical thematic has inhaled the realisation of this artistic work.

It is, as a matter of fact, a stony Bible miniatured and if the robbery could take away from the ancestral soil the grace of the scriptorium worked by the monastery, there stood as sentry of the same, even during the years when the weeds sucket the belly of the fallen stones of the collapsed bulk as unbeatable sentry and eloquent reproduction of the stony Bible, the unpatched porch of Santa Maria.

GUIDEBOOK
Gerona, Spain

For the convenience of patrons, cars will not be hired between November and April.

HOTEL NOTICE
Moscow

See our prices and feel yourselves at home.

BEACH CAFÉ NOTICE
Majorca

Photographs against the bestial seriousness
To press the button in the right moment
Animal photographs cause smilling
Chest hits
Slapstick

PHOTOGRAPHER'S BROCHURE
Munich

In case of fire in your bedroom, keep one's head and do not shout 'FIRE.' Close your door without falling into a panic.

HOTEL NOTICE
Le Havre, France

**Skiers must all be raped on
before crossing the pass**

Cable-car notice
Zermatt, Switzerland

Les Lecheuses Professor Rhesus trought out from his laboratory Maria. Because she makes erotic frolies during her work, she promise to revenge herself. Max, Maria's lover, rob professor Rhesus traught, but when Max gives the traught to somebody the voice is transforming. Max makes a mistakes, he gives the drog to the sister of John his boss and also gangster's thief. At last all finish in the joy.

Publicity leaflet
from French
film company

Young Partridge Over Sofa
Marseilles the Foot Package
Meat Between the Ribs to Trim

MENU ITEMS
Nimes, France

This chair is 'the new thing.' It's new.

The patient in the position from 90 to 0 degrees will not need to move since he will not move his body a single inch. Therefore the Dentist can work undisturbed, without worrying about the Patient.

To obtain all the possible advantages during the work, both standing and sitting to leave the side where the Dentist is working free from the impediment of the which would disturb the approaching to the Patient and to work with the spinal column in vertical position, without physical effort of harmful torsions of the body.

The chair has a unique patented headrest in that its movements allow any position for the patient's head. Patients do not feel insecure. The headrest allows lateral movements of the patient's head – it can be rotated 360°.

Advertisement for
dentist's chair
Turin, Italy

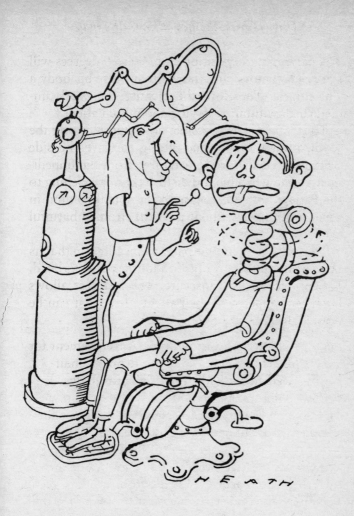

INSTRUCTIONS FOR CUSTOMS DECLARATIONS

Foreign visitors may import ready and conditioned wearing apparel for his use, printed matter for his reading and papers for his writing, articles for his playing and sport exercise, musical instruments which he knows how to play, quantity of food and drinks needed during his trip provided the articles are in compatibilness with his social position.

Passengers with other effects must declare them and pass through the door of the signal lamp.

CUSTOMS NOTICE
Ankara, Turkey

Syrene Bellevue Hotel joins a modern functional equipment with a distinguished and smart style of the 18th century.

It is located vertically on the sea, far off the centre a few minutes afoot and owing to a number of gardens and sunny terraces, guarantee is given for an ideal stay in stillness and absolute rest. The restaurant salon with a large view of the Gulf of Naples, a restaurant service with a big choice, the private beach to be reached by a lift from inside directly, complete the undiscussable peculiarities of the unit.

HOTEL BROCHURE
Sorrento, Italy

Entrance refused to
ladies in bare arms
and gentlemen in knickers

CATHEDRAL NOTICE
Crema, Italy

Ladies in shorts
and gentlemen with naked torsos
are invited to forbid themselves
to enter the Church

CHURCH NOTICE
French Pyrenees

The kilometre '0' of the way of Argent road is in Merida and goes along Caceres, Salamanca, Zamora and ends at Astorga. Roman road that I say at first, It begins in this August Emerita and with every roman constructions is the admiration of all future civilisations up to the present time.

Ways, bridges, theatres are the whole of an Empire and it wonder us. The name of the road is up to date a small mistery and we could attribute it to Arabs people with the constraction of the word BALAT pavement it is, way, they wanted to appoint it the best way, as a manner of administrations for roman people.

PARADOR BROCHURE
Merida, Spain

PLEASE CONTROL YOUR CHANGE!
Remarks doing afterwards should
not be acknowledged

RESTAURANT CASH-DESK NOTICE
Hamburg, West Germany

The traffic and parking of vehicles must be done according to rules of the road and keeper's informations: neither motor horns nor popping bach.

The traffic of motorcars is forbidden after XI pm; motorbicycles will be taken in to hand with their stopped engines.

CAMPSITE INSTRUCTIONS
Vendée river, France

A Half Cock of the Countrywoman
Rum Steak and Ships

HOTEL MENU ITEMS
Paris

THE GRASS YOU MUST NOT MARCH ON HIM

PARK NOTICE
Brussels

The choiced songs will be presented in the Festival by the exponents designed by the same Commission, being able the respectives authors to propose names of possible exponents, under pretext purely informative of the Commission of the Festival, this being not an obligation to same to accept its trade.

SONG FESTIVAL RULES
Spain

F/D 220-C/2 is the best fitted machine for the modern requirements of the Alimentary Industry.

By her numerous performances, she gives entire satisfaction; besides her dosimeter of a new and modern, invention, permits a continuance of work, keeping constant the gram-measure even with mixtures on a fowl extract basis.

The accuracy in the choice of the construction materials, the assembly of the movements on ball-bearings and bronze bushings, the total and coustant lubrification – as its is automatic and forced – make the machine noiseless and long lasting.

A contrivance, of an easy move, permits to isolate an to exclude, at the same time, the whole dosing group in order to permit the cleaning operation and the change of the paper bobbin.

Packing machinery sales brochure
Milan, Italy

If service required give two strokes to the maid and three for the varlet.

Notice by hotel
room bell-push
Austria

The Rules on Utilization of Accommodation

To maintain the generality and reliability of the hotel, the guests are requested to observe the following rules. In case one of these rules is violated by a certain guest, his or her stay will be discontinued.

Not to give annoyance to the others by making a great noise or disgusting behaviors.

Not to carry the followings in to the room or the hallway

(A) Animals, Birds, etc.
(B) Things with loathsome smell
(C) Items of great quantity
(D) Explosive items such as powder, gasoline, etc.
(E) Illegally owned guns and swords

Not to gamble or beheve in a demoralizing manner in this hotel.

Not to bring visitors into the room and let them use the furnitures and fixtures without a sufficient cause.

Not to use the furnitures and fixtures in the room or the hall-way for the purpose other than the original object.

Not to throw the things from the window of the guest's room.

HOTEL NOTICE
Tokyo

WERY STRONK BIER

BAR NOTICE
Finland ferry

The grissino is prepared in the COLAG bakery with the most modern engines and dy skilled worckers. It is known for its high nourishing power. Its freshness and friability, the genuine row materials are a warranty of easy digestibility. It is recomended as a nourishment for children, grown up people and aged persons.

GRISSINI BREAD WRAPPER
Italy

PLEASE DO NOT BRING SOLICITORS INTO YOUR ROOM

HOTEL ROOM NOTICE
Chinag-Mai,
Thailand

The country's agents stamped on the backside will carry out the honour of the guarantee in their country.

Akai tape-recorder
guarantee

The Town of Pamplona greets you and is pleased with your visit at the present Festivities of St. Fermin, and sincerely wishes that you will enjoy yourselves.

We hope to have your collaboration to spend the time in harmony with the Authorities and refrain from all actions so as to adjust the real meaning of our festivities.

For your information, we show two very important aspects in relation with the Festivities of St. Fermin.

1 "WHAT YOU CAN DO FOR ST. FERMIN"

- To have a good time within the proper limits of the festivities, and to be exact according to your education, and to have respect, and above all to be civil.
- To form groups in order to manifest cheerfulness, taking instruments to give animation in the streets of the town.
- To assist in all the acts of that which is organized, publicy or privalety in co-operation with the normal established rules, and instructions to indicate the responsibility or the Agents of the Municipal Police.
- To direct people in the conditions as it ought to be with the adequate education to denote the correction, and respect all the time.

- To utilize public establishments with the correct education, using food with the conditions peoper to its use, without causing any prejudice.
- Intervention in the general ambient of the festivities presented in so far as it ought to be, that is, where personal clean clothing is concerned.

2 "WHAT YOU MUST NOT DO"

- To walk around alone or in groups, in an inadequate form and adapting attitudes that denote a personal bad state, to offend the elemental civil conduct.
- To be in an intoxicated state, a punishment can be imposed in case of committing some act punishable.
- To make noises and scandals in the sight of the public and establishments.
- Sit down or lie down in sight of the public, to obstruct the freedom and movement of people.
- To make public or scenes which are supposed to be against moral and good customs.
- To behave badly in any form to people, particulary, to a woman.
- Causing damage to property and food instalations in the sight of the public.
- Utilizing ponds, fountains, for personal use.
- To cross or tread the green zones or gardens of the town.
- To break or tear objects in sight of the public or crowded places.

- To camp in places that are not expressly authorised.
- To park cars in bad conditions or in places that are prohibited.
- To drive too fast or in a reckless manner.
- To utilize percussion instruments after Midnight.

3   THE RUNNING BEFORE THE BULLS AND BULL SQUARE

- Situated in prohibited zones, disobeying the orders of the Agents of the Authority.
- Calling the attention of the bulls in any manner.
- Running in the sense contrary to the direction of the bulls.
- To stay in the enclosure is difficult for the defense of the runners.
- Running or staying in the running of the bulls in an intoxicated state, or appearing in inadequate clothing.
- Stopping in the way, difficult for the race of the runners.
- Causing difficulties in any manner normally obstructing the runners.
- To hold down and to hit the cows and bulls in Bull Square or in the bull ring.

HANDBILL
Pamplona, Spain

Little Joes of Jam
Warm Calf to the Sap
Warms Little Dogs
Combinated of Assaulted Greengroceries
Fillet of Backs Pig to the Metalplatte
  or Cooked in Past
Roasted Jam to the American Style
Fried Eggs in Torttle or Restless

MENU ITEMS
Athens

TRAVEL INTERNATIONAL

offers

Domestic flights round the world TODAY

International flights to Moon TOMORROW

And Moon to Mars DAY AFTER

NEWSPAPER ADVERTISEMENT
Bangladesh

When a dish has rum out of the Plate of the Day for ani circunstance the client wull de entirely to choose any other dish for the some group of the card, even-thouth the said dish without surcharge being added to the price of the plate of the day.

MENU CARD
Madrid

44

It is forbidden to couple all kinds of electrical contrivances (shaving machines excluded) like electric iron, kettle or similar object to the network of lighting, and the employ of the current of lighting for other than the own lamps of the house is absolutely forbidden.

HOTEL ROOM NOTICE
Helsinki

The sun usually rises on the eastern side of the rock.

TOURIST BROCHURE
Gibraltar

We lie in the mountains near the Salzkammergut lakes with lots of snow in winter at a height of about 4,200 feet.

In summer our aero is specially adiguate for people that want to necreate.

HOTEL PRESS RELEASE
Austria

The broiled sausages are only being made from the ham meat and by roasting on the grid they have got along with them the good taste of hard wood fire.

Both cold and hot (frying them slightly in a hot pan, with a bit of pure hog's grease) they taste really very good.

BRATWURST PACK
West Germany

ACT 1   Carmen is a cigar-makeress from a tabago factory who loves with Don Jose of the mounting guard. Carmen takes a flower from her corsets and lances it to Don Jose (Duet: *Talk me of my mother*).

There is a noise inside the tabago factory and the revolting cigar-makeresses burst into the stage. Carmen is arrested and Don Jose is ordered to mounting guard her but Carmen subduces him and he lets her escape.

ACT 2   The Tavern. Carmen, Frasquito, Mercedes, Zuniga, Morales. Carmen's aria (*The sistrums are tinkling*). Enter Escamillio, a balls-fighter. Enter two smuglers (Duet: *We have in mind a business*) but Carmen refuses to penetrate because Don Jose has liberated her from prison.

He just now arrives (Aria: *Slop, here who comes!*) but hear are the bugles singing his retreat. Don Jose will leave and draws his sword. Called by Carmen shrieks the two smuglers interfere with her but Don

Jose is bound to dessert, he will follow into them (final chorus: *Opening sky wandering life*).

ACT 3   A roky landscape, the smuglers shelter. Carmen sees her death in cards and Don Jose makes a date with Carmen for the next balls fight.

ACT 4   A place in Seville. Procession of balls-fighters, the roaring of the balls is heard in the arena. Escamillio enters (Aria and chorus: *Toreador, toreador, All hail the balls of a Toreador*).
  Enter Don Jose (Aria: *I do not threaten, I besooch you*) but Carmen repels him wants to join with Escamillio now chaired by the crowd. Don Jose stabbs her (Aria: *Oh rupture, rupture, you may arrest me, I did kill her*) he sings *Oh my beautiful Carmen, my subductive Carmen*.

OPERA HOUSE PROGRAMME
Genoa, Italy

Aeroflot Soviet Airlines has more than 100,000 miles of international airlines, disposing of the latest aircraft and equipment and experienced pilots and personnel.

AIRPORT NOTICE
Leningrad, USSR

Your car is wrongly parked. In a few moments it will be taken to the Police Station and bound up.

WINDSCREEN NOTICE
St. Tropez, France

Looking the meander and the high acclivous streets, you can imagen the soul of the corsaires running away from the old braved settlers.

The old houses silent witness of the history, still restless to the pass of the ages, steps and stonewalls talk about history and reflex mistery.

GUIDEBOOK
La Guaira, Venezuela

SEEK

I have mind to have a pharmacist or a chemist for my wife, who can converse in more than 2 languages and is from age 22 to 26, and can give secret aid to my medical study. Self-introduction.

I am a physician of Japan, 27 years old and in the serve of certain public hospital. I look forward to be sent me your personal history with photogrph by you.

NEWSPAPER ADVERTISEMENT
Amsterdam

Flying water in all room. You may bask in sin on patio.

HOTEL NOTICE
Istanbul

You will make a trip in the steppes and have optic appearances.

TRAVEL BROCHURE
Sweden

When you dine at the 'Metro' restaurant you will have the feeling you are being literally wafted up to heaven. when you take the first bite of a *cotelette de volaille* stuffed with pasty.

As for the *tripe à la polpetta* which will be served you at the Hotel Monopol. . .you will be singing its praises to your grandchildren as you lie on your deathbed.

And then again, somewhere, sometime, you may be given a *tenderloin à la Châteaubriand* tough as a pine lath; well, then, you break your teeth, and so, without teeth and hungry you go off to bed.

Whatever you may meet up with, one thing we can positively guarantee – YOU WILL NOT BE BORED IN POLAND! POLAND IS THE COUNTRY FOR GREAT EXPERIENCES!

TOURIST BROCHURE
Poland

Emperor Akbar reigned for 49 years peacefully, but his later days were saddenly by the ill-conduct of his son Salim, who revelled against his father and killed Akbar's fast friend Abul Fazal.

Emperor Jehangir had 7,000 ladies in the harem. As he was a talented drunkard and a luxurious man he died in 1627 at the age of 57 years.

GUIDEBOOK
Agra, India

The way to use the telephone differs from town to town. It will be necessary to inquire beforehand. In most cases you will be able to ask somebody to connect you with the wanted number. If that is possible you better don't fail to do so.

Excuse me, Sir! *Maaf, Tuan!*

I'm 'strange with' telephoning. *Saja 'belum biasa' menelepon.*

'Will you' connect me with Bandung 4162? *'Sudikah Tuan' menjambung saja dengan Bandung: empat, satu, enam, dua?*

In case you are forced to help yourself, and the telephone is not automatic, you should ask the operator to connect you with the wanted 'district' first, i.e. when you are in an other district.

Then tell the number, calling the ciphers one by one:

1=*satu*   2=*dua*   3=*tiga*   4=*empat*   5=*lima*
6=*enam*   7=*tudjuh*   8=*delapan*   9=*sembilan*
0=*nol.*

Call the operator *Nona* (=Miss) when you hear she is a girl. Don't call a male-operator anything.

Thus hearing from the tone of the opening *Halo!* (=Hullo) that the operator's sex is all right, you say:

Tolong sambung dengan . . . Bandung . . . empat . . . satu . . . enam . . . dua . . . Nona! (with a musical stress on the last syllable). = Please connect me with . . . etc.!

She, knowing her work, will repeat plainly: '4162'

so plainly that it is impossible to write the digits down in letters!

Still your voice should remain appealing. Stick to that!

Betul, Nona! = 'Correct, Miss Operator!' Of course, only in case that it *is* correct. If not:

Bukan, Nona! (repeating) *Bandung . . . empat . . . satu . . .* etc., still appealing after every repetition. . .

Take a seat.

The operators are very, very busy; don't push on! In case you lose your temper, the operator will connect you with a nasty colleague.

From *The Traveller's Lexicon* published in Bandung, Indonesia

Salad with gardener
Rock soup
Arm of a Gipsy
Saints bones

MENU ITEMS
Madrid

Children Sandwiches

MENU ITEM
Copenhagen

Your luminous name glorifies a precious bottle. Your nectar – gay and happy son of old and noble race – comes from the ancient stub of provincial soil and matures in an elating sun.

WINE BOTTLE LABEL
Cannes, France

For the regulation of central articulation, take the lever and the screw in houry direction the ring so is rapresented on the illustration. Screw now the lever till required constraining.

TABLE-LAMP INSTRUCTIONS
Spain

**The grave of Karl Marx
Highgateski Cemetery, London, England**

POSTCARD CAPTION
Moscow

NOT TO TOUCH!
TRANSGRESSORS WILL BE REFERRED
TO THE JUDICIAL AUTHORITY!

Notice in
St Mark's Cathedral
Venice, Italy

Mr. Emmanuel Marnieros together with wis sons Dimitri and Mihali are at any time at your disposition in order to satisfy all whichever if your desires.

A staff carefully chocen – cooks, waiters and artists – will be occupied with you, in order clients to excellently served.

And the children? A great infant joy – Balances, Trambolins, sliders, are at their disposition.

The gooses-lake, a more idulic coin, as well for great ans small. Sun, green, and a pure atmosphere, ideal place for real relapse.

After lunch, coffee and the play-cards arrangement in the special drawing-room are offering new emotions.

The wines are of the owner's property but you can as well ask for other sorts of spirits and refreshements of your preference.

Amusements, danse, parties till morning, throug entraining orchestras.

Unforgotten moments of fun, amusements and danse on the pista.

RESTAURANT BROCHURE
Kifissia, Greece

The hour will be 60 minutes late today.

TIME ZONE WARNING
Italian cruise ship

54

Eggs with a Reindeer
Grained Pike-perch with Much Rooms
Cock in Red Wine
Shanghai Sailors Chicke Curry

MENU ITEMS
Turku, Finland

From Hotel GIARDINI you Will Find familiarity facilities and elegance.

This huose offers its guests every modern commodity to meet with all their exigencies, as hot and cold running water, intern telephone in every room, central heasting.

Big dining-room, restaurant, Bar, reading and conversation-room, dancing and concert-room with notorious band; shady Garden; cellar supplied with all sorts of exquisit drinks and liquors.

HOTEL BROCHURE
Chiavari, Italy

Dear Guest
On September 30, winter timing will start. As of 12:00 midnight all clocks will be forward one hour back.
Truly yours,
The Management

HOTEL NOTICE
Cairo

If the ship sinks walk quickly to the liferafts.
Do not swim

> Notice, Bosphorus
> pleasure steamer

Please do not put heavy bodies
into the washbasin

> Notice, Belgian
> cross-Channel ferry

Passengers are required to disembark
in orderly manner and not
to drink the water

> Notice, pleasure
> boat, Cairo

When the stewards dance, please
do not throw plates at them

> Notice, Greek
> cruise ship

Nestcafe
Zin
French Likers
Gingerel
Orange Tuice
Blandy Mary
Other licferent drings
Polls with Jams of Spoon
Tartars
Cucunmlbers
Beef Roots

BAR TARIFF
Hydra, Greece

AMERICAN RESTAURANT

Peking Will-known Menu Chinese
& Western Excellent Wines Potlucks
Ordinary Meals of Your Own Accord Peking
Pastry and Puddings Specialist in Roast Chickens
Sanitary Equipments Hospitable Waiters You Are
Welcome to Telephone Orders Prompt Attendance

RESTAURANT SIGN
Hong Kong

Extract of fowl, poached or sunside up

MENU ITEM
France

SEA LIFE

Prepared Slides

1 Placoid Scale of Dogfish
  This is the extremely same structure as that of teeth. Parts in the skin spread out like a mortar.
2 Cycloid Scale of Sardine
  This looks like the annual ring of a tree. The scale grows up as one grows older.
3 Spicule of Sea-Cucumber
  There are many kind of spicule pattern depending on the assortments. Therefore, maniac for collecting Spicules will be captivated.
4 Gloiopeltis Complanata
  This is one of seaweeds.
5 Pandina Arborescens
  This is the brown algae that lives gregariously in the tide-drift.
6 Egg of Shrimp
  Shrimp tastes good as for food and also it is one of the important fisher sources as it can be taken much. Shrimp that got out of an egg repeats casting off several times and grows up.

Leaflet with
microscope slides
Japan

HOTEL CHICAGO

Grand, entirely renovated.
All roms with balconies, running water, central heating, shower, telephones, Buffer, Wating room and in general, all modern comforts for a confortable residence.

LOGICAL PRICES
CIVILISATION   DIGNITY   CLEANLINESS

HOTEL ADVERTISEMENT
Piraeus, Greece

The telegraph and telephone regie demands from its staff the greatest obligingness and service with respect to the clientelle.

Customers are asked to contribute to the easiness of the personals task.

Any complaints should be recorded in the box wich is at the customer's disposal at the counter.

POST OFFICE NOTICE
Brussels

Don't leave the path to pick flowers; you risk a deadly fall or glide.

HOTEL NOTICE
Switzerland

Leaving the room (has to takplace) up til
12.00 – noon. The hotel management is not
deposited with the reception official.

A land where nature with its voluptuous
beauty and human creativity with its marvellous achievements have succeeded in creating
a felicitous ensemble which constitutes a kind
of glorification.

Jerked Meat
Fumigated Sausage
Fried Chinken
Hunragien Veal Collops
Dumlings Samlo Styl
Zingarakewers

Fried mouses in Vanille Sauce

MENU ITEM
Kitzbuhel, Austria

Important: Albadoro Cannelloni do not ought to boil.

1 Bring in Cannelloni, as they are, a stuffing maked with: beef, eggs, cheese, parmigiano, papper or spices, as you like, all well amalgamated ad juicy.

2 Besmear a backing-pan, previously buttered, with a good tomato-sauce and after, dispose the Cannelloni, lightly distanced between them, in a only couch.

At last, for a safe success in cooking, shed the remnant sauce, possibly diluted with broth, as far as to cover the surface of Cannelloni.

3 Add puffs of butter and grated cheese, cover the backing-pan, and put her into the over, previously warmed at 180/200 centigrade degrees above zero.

4 Cook for about half of hour at the same temperature without to uncover the backing-pan and after, to help at table.

COOKING INSTRUCTIONS
Pack of cannelloni

FIRE!   It is what can doing we hope. No fear. Not ourselves. Say quickly to all people coming up down everywhere a prayer. Always is a clerk. He is assured of safety by expert men who are in the bar for telephone for the fighters of the fire come out.

HOTEL BEDROOM NOTICE
Rome

Jelly Belly, Tailor
Please, No. 2 Missee want you trousis

IT IS DEFENDED TO PROMENADE THE
CORRIDORS IN THE BOOTS OF
THE MOUNTAIN IN FRONT
OF SEVEN HOURS

To work please pull chain wait a bit please pull chain wait a bit please pull chain two times and see fresh cascade.

If this is your first visit to the USSR, you are welcome to it.

For those in search of the savour of experiences that are all the dearer because they seem so irrevocably part of the past, the moment has come to stop and look around. Immersed in the perfume of quaint essences, in the strange light between magic and reality, discover this handful of earth and granite: Calabria!

Its strong and harsh aspect, of unexpected and incredible loveliness at times, induces those who speak of it to do so in a hushed voice. Its countenance, though maintaining the aristocratic features of those that for generations have not bent their heads, bears the signs of long inner suffering and is all the more beautiful for it.

Eternal movement of the sea with its infinite shades of turquoise and blue and purple, sharp cliffs, velvety sand, fragrance and bergamots and jasmine – stunning and evocative of past amours – sharp rocks, dense woods that open into small lakes as a maiden would open her shy eyes, fresh and evergreen citrus orchards with their golden fruit, haughty olive trees, evocative, in the silver of their foliage, of those grandfathers who still know the stories of olden times: Calabria!

TOURIST OFFICE BROCHURE
Calabria, Italy

Gentlemen are requested to wear long socks and singlet.

HOTEL DINING-ROOM SIGN
Darwin, Australia

Curled Milka Sleep

MENU ITEM
Greece

FABULOUS BELLY DANGER FROM ISTANBUL

RESTAURANT ADVERTISEMENT
Nicosia, Cyprus

The concessionaire of the services of sweepings collection. . .request that, in profit of the cleanliness, must be taken into consideration the following ends:

That the collection of sweepings is made during the night, since 12 hours, daily, except Saturdays night, because Sundays is not given this service, so, it is important that the pails and bags are situated in very visible places, before 12 hours of the night.

PUBLIC NOTICE
Denia, Spain

Come you have a drink free!
Holy Wine – a special kind of white raisins, otted in the last time of autumn, sun maid on mats of dried grass and when they are reasing, they will be caved in the Week of Silence.

SUPERMARKET LEAFLET
Riva, Italy

1 – Insert medical preparation into atomizer's ampulla (2) through the opening with gum-stopper;
2 – Insert other gum tube's end in atomizer-ampulla's hole (x);
3 – Connect muff (D) to atomizer's ampulla's hole (y), then to mouth-pipe (3), or nose-fork (4), or gum-marsk (5), according to applications to be effected (illustration 2);
4 – Place atomizer's ampulla in right seat (B);
5 – Insert plug (C) in contact-box and press inter-rupter (A).

BY ENDED EROGATION PUT IMMEDIATELY APPARATUS OUT.

Bronchial atomiser
instructions
Italy

French widow in every room.

HOTEL BROCHURE
Switzerland

ATHENS: The city that revive with his anciens tombs, and the immortal Greek civilization from deepest century's under his blue sky.

STREET MAP
Athens

RULES TO KEEP IN THIS PLACE

We call this place MONKEY PALADISE because there about more than thirty monkies are left free in this place.

These monkies live according to their wild nature since they are kept for ecological observation purpose, even though they are tamed to people.

Please keep the following rules in order to prevent accidents caused by offensive treatments against monkies' nature.

We can not be responsible for your accidents happened by disregarding these rules.

LET'S OBEY INSTRUCTIONS IN CHARGE AND KEEP FIVE DONT'S

1 Don't touch monkies.
   If you do so, they will bite or scratch you, mis-understanding that you are going to catch.
2 Don't close your face to monkies.
   For monkies, closing face means 'threat.'
3 Don't tease monkies.

They will be mad and pounce on you if you pat or shout.
4 Don't show your fruits.
If you do so, they will steal from you, thinking that you have brought food for them.
5 Don't leave younger children walk about alone.

**TAKAO MOUNTAIN RAILWAY COMPANY
JAPAN WILD MONKIES PROTECTION CLUB**

PUBLIC NOTICE
Japan

Certified midwife: entrance sideways

STREET SIGN
Jerusalem, Israel

Shrimp Nets
Guttlefish
Bing Breams
Sqabs
Hen Blood Stew
Quince Past
Slop Brandy

MENU ITEMS
Oporto, Portugal

If set breaks, inform manager. Do not interfere with yourself.

Island of small size, but with great variety of land-scapes, and the visitor will enjoy discovering by himself so in villages, and in several places of coast, too.

Main towns are ten, smiling, white and harbourer, but each one with well definite characters.

As this bath tub overflow pipe has a air hole thereby when you full the tub with water, kindly allow after you got in the tub the water level is below the overflow pipe – otherwise the water will run inside the bathroom floor.

ARRANGEMENT FOR THE CAMPING-SITE

Enact of the Home Office
of Baden-Wurttemberg
No. X 2078/20 in the Official Gazette
No. 12, page 213/214

No. 1 A pretension to utilisation does not exist. All kinds of tramps are not admitted. The practice of ambulatory trade or shows on the camping site are forbidden.

No. 2 At his arrival each user has to register into an entry-form, showing his identitly-card. Until the payment a legitimation can be held back.

No. 3 The fees for the utilization of the site agree with the actually valuable arrangement of fees.

No. 4 The watchman of the camping site indicates the camping spot.

No. 5 The mutual passing the night in a tent is only permitted to married people or parents with their children. An offence against this arrangement is punished by immediate expulsion. Moreover young people will be denounced at the competent juvenile court in order to inform the persons of their education.

No. 6 All users of the site to behave themselves

corresponding the allbountiful rules of good address and morals and to dress decently. The washing machine in the laundry may only be used in presence of the ward woman. Therefore we ask the adults not to let the little children go to the WC alone.

Motor vehicles shall only drive by steps inside the camping site. Herewith it is forbidden to surround a tent by a drain.

No. 7 During the camping stay take care of cleanness and order. Put refuse into the boxes at hand.

No. 8 It is forbidden to bring dogs with one.

No. 9 Molestations by noise, particular by radios, loud singing, practising music and shouting are to forbear. The volume of sound (of radios) is to limit.

Extracts from
campsite regulations
Kirchzarten, West Germany

Frozen Soup with Peccadilloes

MENU ITEM
Marbella, Spain

Please use the telephone for ALL calls

Hotel bedside
telephone notice
Segovia, Spain

In case of emergency, say No.

Hotel bedside
telephone notice
Leipzig, East Germany

Please follow cautiously your safety instructions as an entertainment more in your flight.

Do not hesitate to ask any questions you have about its interpretation.

On an Emergency during this flight, you will be precisely instructed about what you should do.

Do not forget the crew members are accurately trained experts.

Please, follow the instructions you receive and above all keep quiet!

Many Thanks!

Safety instruction leaflet
Iberia International
Airlines of Spain

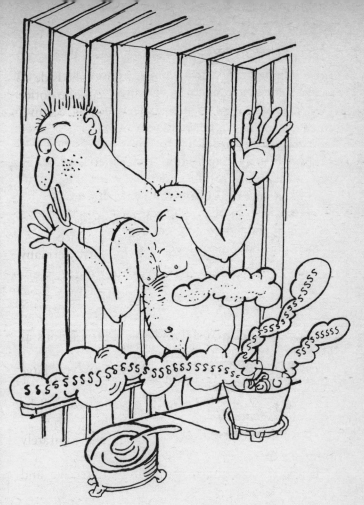

Why not try out our sauna baths? If you are lucky you might get a hot sausage.

HOTEL NOTICE
Rovaniemi, Finland

This product shall not be used on kept at a high or low temperature environment. Especially, never leave it for long time under the direct rays of the sun. When it was kept in a high temperature environment, there may appear a long Newton's rings (interference fringes) from left to right in the center part of the display panel. But it does not mean any inferiority of the product. When it was put again in a normal temperature environment, the interference fringes will disappear and return to the former state. As this phenomenon does not mean any change in its function, so use it with feeling at ease.

Electronic game
instructions, Japan

We are informed of many miscarriages during the sending of information and propaganda materiel. If the one announced by us with the present letter did not arrive to you timely, write us, please, we will repeat the sending.

Tourist office letter
Italy

The Proprietor does not speak English but is very obliginging.

SHOP-WINDOW NOTICE
Majorca

Dear Madam,

We regret to inform you that the grey flowered silk dress and jacket for clean on the 30th March, was damaged by the water dropping from the upstairs, in which our upstairs is Carnarvon Hotel, who's passenger forgot short the water, therefore, until early morning the water coming and happen dripping down to our full place and whole clothes was wet and damaged, however, we are unfortunate in this matter of lot customer's garment was so much damaged by the way. Under this circumstance.

We beg to your kind consideration and forgive us for our unfortunate! May we dyeing it into black colour or not?

Expecting you for your kindness, we remain,
Very truly yours,

Letter from dry cleaners
Hong Kong

What offer the civilisation beside the nature? The animals let see in the fresh morning – and cool evening-hours. Out the Naab-waves snap gasp for breath pines and eels.

CAMPSITE NOTICE
Piesport, West Germany

A sports jacket may be worn to dinner but no trousers.

We always serve tea in bag like mother.

MENU CARD
Lloret, Spain

No bags served here

TEAROOM NOTICE
Lido de Jesolo, Italy

NADER'S HOTLE

The International Hotel at Embassies Area, Khartoum No. 1 Street No. 1 West Khartoum International Airport, and South United Arab Club at Khartoum No. 1.

Airconditioned Rooms, Imported Furniture and locally from Eissa Ahmed Khalil.

An International Waiting Room and Dining One too, nice services complete, and available transport.

A Big attractive Garden for receiptions and also an excellent Roof Garden and calm.

HANDBILL
Khartoum, Sudan

The Management is not responsible for valu-
ables unless such are deposited in the hotel
safe, which is open between 7.00 and 20.00.

HOTEL NOTICE
Stockholm

NO NUDE BATHING PERMITTED
EXCEPT UNDER SUPERVISION OF
MANAGEMENT

POOLSIDE NOTICE
Long Island NY, USA

PROFILE OF SINTRA

by Candido Luis

Very often we say that the choises of touristic
markets are directed to the sun and the sea. Now,
well, at Sintra there isn't only a touristic sense.
Actually, we can say that the tendency spreads
between the green and tuffy mountains and the
golden beaches that enlarge along the coast.

All the large municipality offers magnificent ambi-
ents of local merits, since the folk up to beauty of the
building and embellishment and amenity of the
weather all the year long, and also the abundant,
healthy and agreable meals.

SINTRA BOLETIM
Portugal

There is no stopping Mr Luis. Here he is again . . .

HAIL, SINTRA!

by Candido Luis

If you get to her belvederes of an extraordinary beauty and if you glance at the wonderful sights, you will admit Sintra is the perfect place to take care of neurosis caused by a feverish and exciting life.

If you go on the hill and if you remain along with that singular Nature, whose corcery disturbs the most insensible man, in a circle where you feel the noises' delivery you will know the good ambient where you are.

VISITOR'S NEWSPAPER
Portugal

In case of claim
let us join this ticket
But if you are pleased
Let us make known and
require the taste of
altitude Golden
VERGERS du LIMOUSIN

APPLE-CARTON LABEL
Perigueux, France

81

PETIZERS
Antzougies
Eggs of Fish Salat

BOILINGS
Calf
Head ½
Brains salat

FISHES
Sfiris boiling
Sfiris fried
Porcies
Sguid fried
Tuna fieh
Makerel greele

BLUSHING
Poure

LAMP WITH PASTRY
Pof coast

CALF WITH PASTRY
Sqoosh

CHOPPED MEATS
Pastitzio
Meats ball
Rece with choped M
Bowels

ROAST MEATS
Little Lamp
Head Lamp

ON TIME
Geaps of Lamp Greece
Steks of Calf
Meats Ball Greele
Liver fried of Calf

OLIES
Gumpoes
Poure
Beans dry
Beans Giant
Chick Peast

SALADS
Beet roots garlic

CHEESE
Rok For

SPECIALITY
Calf dish
Lamp Milk Country
Fried Meat Ball ala Russian
Kanelonia ala Toscan

COMPOSTES
Plum
Apricot

MENU
Piraeus, Greece

83

**All the tickets for the train
to Tokyo are soiled.**

STATION NOTICE
Kyoto, Japan

Insert a money of 5 or 10 lire and presse deeply the
stud.

PAPER TOWEL MACHINE
Montecatini-Terme, Italy

The comfortable day bar, with its terrace over the
valley where everybody feels himself in private, is
appreciated by elderly people.
 After daylight, the evening bar, where music can
not be heard in other parts of the castle, receives
youngs and olders in a good relaxing atmosphere.

Letter from a
French hotel
manager

MARMALADE

Ingredients: Sugar Oranges Conservatives

JAR LABEL
Hong Kong

84

Because of the impropriety of entertaining guests of the opposite sex in the bedroom, it is suggested that the lobby be used for this purpose.

HOTEL NOTICE
Zurich

La Scaletta

Only a few monts have not been enough to grow for the entry pergola being typical of the Italian inns which are noted in their agendas by the foreign tourists aiming to describe them on their return. As well as the good smelling mysteries of egg noodles, which replace here *trenette al pesto* have been learned within a short time. Mrs. Maria boasts that wines and raw food are genuine at all.

Alhambra dancing

It is not an important matter for the visitors of the Club that the town is placed at the mouth of the Valley of the Magra, at the foot of Armello; they are much more interested to the milieu, service and whisky and cognac brands. At any rate, nothing is more probable than to find at *Alhambra* some people who come and look for a new sport overtime, after admiring long time the most suggestive spots in the outskirts.

Zena bathing-establishment

When chosing a bathing-establishment, take in account those of them which close their gates on sunset but open after the dinner, all the members of the family would be satisfied. Also due to the reason people always like rather to allow their boys and girls to be free if the milieu they have dances (fashion actually orders dances to be many thousands) is well known. Confortable huts and faithful customers.

Carmarino

They who have been acquainted with these spots in summer must be ready to see them later under some different points of view. But Nino Carmarino's shop will never deceive them; the shop is always renewed in its assortment, just up-to-date, even if the offered suits will suggest a distrustful contact with the most adverse nature. The winter season at the sea submits unhoped suggestions for grown-up people and children in its own fashion.

Lorenzelli

Even if the most assortment consists of hoisieries (fashion has actually overpassed the boundaries of cities and, wherever you can find 'new' and also very successful at competitive prices), at *Lorenzelli's* you can buy gent's and lady's clothes of good brand, as well as, of course, lambswool and shetland in the most fashionable colours.

Luciani

All the performances of a refined boutique. Day and evening dresses, *tailleurs* covercoats, in addition to all the co-ordinated which seem to be unnecessary (never useless, of course) before buying. Their guidebook at hands there are people who arrive, in summer and winter, to visit Lunigiana's castles and leave once again with a trasparent and impalpable evening-blouse of high couture.

Sporting plants
Bowling: course (the lighting plant is going on to be built)
Basketball: stadium (going on to be prepared)
Volleyball: stadium (going on to be prepared)
Skating: 2 racks, the latter under preparation
Tennis: some lawns (going on to be prepared)

From the guidebook *Liguria: How and Were*, published in Genoa, Italy

We will embark for the island of Lobos, where we will have plenty of time to have a swim and to admire the marines' bottoms.

TOURIST BROCHURE
Tenerife

If you wash same dish that don came in this menu you can ask for the lunch's menu.

If one or more dish be finished on the day menu you can choice another of similar caracteristic without any suplemen charge.

MENU CARD
Madrid

DO NOT PARKING

The crane will attack your vehicle

DOCKS NOTICE
Barcelona, Spain

Yee Tai Ziang Ivory Co.

We cleator the ivory thing for artiful. As the pencane, Fambone, Smoke Beak, Tobbacco Purse, Ivory Bell, Penturb, Printcase and Article the Singnature and other things. There has a great number names that could not point in here if you would trading with Me. We Would Gave You The Low Price.

BUSINESS CARD
Shanghai, China

Bismark with Hindrance
Clear soup with Pancake Rags

MENU ITEMS
Postojna, Yugoslavia

Visit our bargain basement upstairs

SHOP SIGN
Malta

How old are you?

I shall be five-and-forty the sixth of next July.

You are in the prime of life. You are still a young man. And your nephew?

He is only six years old. He is but a child He is still in his infancy. He is only just born.

Your aunt appears very aged.

She completed her 71st year last month. She has still the hue of health. Would you believe her father is still living?

He must be very old.

He is just entering his 96th year.

It is a fine old age.

He is not yet tired of life. His brother, who is younger than he, is quite decrepit. He is in a state of extreme decay. He has already one foot in the grave. He is at the last gasp. He cannot last much longer. He is like a candle glimmering in the socket.

My eldest sister had the whooping cough, the youngest had the measles, my eldest brother the small-pox and the youngest a military fever.

I sincerely pity your mother; she must have had a great deal of fatigue.

I wish to go to bed directly. Go and turn down my bed.

I will go instantly. Shall I warm your bed?

No, but make a fire in my room for it is very cold.

Everything is ready. You may walk up when you think proper.

Give me my slippers and my nightcap.

Shall I help you to undress?

There is no occasion. Has anyone been here to enquire about me?

There has been a gentleman whom I do not know and who would not leave his name. He said he would call again tomorrow, early.

Don't forget to wind up my watch and put it at the head of my bed.

Do you wish to have a light? The night-lamp is quite ready.

Very well, you may light it before you go. Draw the curtains a little closer that the light may not be troublesome to me.

Is there anything else I can do?

I have drunk more than usual and feel myself a little heated; put a glass of sugar and water upon the night-table.

If you feel indisposed I will sit up with you.

No, no. Go to bed. Besides, if I want anything I will ring for you.

Do you notice that at every instant we feel a very unpleasant jolting?

It is what they call rocking and it rises from some imperfection in the laying of the rails or the construction of the wheels.

There is a fast train coming to meet us. It seems to me it is on our line!

Don't be afraid; the down trains such as ours always go on the left line and the up trains on the right.

We have already passed over several bridges; now we
   are over a viaduct.
It is really frightful; it seems as if we are suspended in
   the air.

From a French-English
phrase-book published
in Paris, 1899

Fogosh Miller's Wife Style
Fried Sheat-Fish with Spawned Cabbage
Noodled Loins in Bull's Blood
Robber's Meat
Spanish Bird
Dzrwed Boans with Pork Meat

MENU ITEMS
Budapest

1 To all hotel assistants, in order to prevent shoes
  from misleying please don't corridor them.
2 The management of this Hotel cannot be held. He
  is responsible for articles deposited to the office
  against receipt.

HOTEL NOTICE
Athens

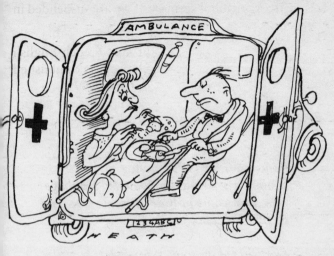

You are invite to visit our restaurant where you can eat the Middle East foods in an European ambulance.

HOTEL NOTICE
Ankara, Turkey

TABU DISCOTEQUE

With or without a date and in summer –
plus open air banging-bar.

POSTER
Torremolinos, Spain

It is defended to circulate the hotel in the boots of the ascension.

Ladies can have fits upstairs.

We buy and we seld stamps and coins. Large selection in spanish stamps and the rest of the world. You can to see us ni your next visit and you will be satisfationed.

Shefish
Ham Higbkander
Egg Fiemush
Srips
Stripe Omelet
Bee Tongue fried
Stuffed pippers
Bluberlips
Frozen Cake

CAMPING REGULATIONS

Forbiden to dig holes to throw residum en el Camping. The encampers must use the Healtful installations and to deposit in places buill to this object the sweepings the place used during the staying will rest perfectly clean at the date of departure.

Not any harm must be done to the Campig install-ations, specialy to the plantations. It's not allowed to drive nails on the trees.

It's forbidden to ligh any wooden fire, for the cooking as well as the camping fires. Only fires or hotter of gaz, alcohol or essence will be authorised.

Perfect and good manners are to be observed. The pieces called 'bath of sun' or slips are not admissible.

The camping direction is not responsible of mater-ials vehicles and other objects borught to the camping by encampers. It's not responsible to in case of fire.

To share the calm and well being of campers the public is not allowed to enter into the camping inclosure for general interest the campers are obliged to observe this rules the unaccomplishment of the same will give place to denunciations to the Governative authorities which shall apply the suit-able sanction.

CAMPING SITE RULES
Benicasim, Spain

WATCHES

SEIKO-QUARTZ
Chrono Anal-Digit   £22.00

DUTY-FREE CATALOGUE
Belgian cross-Channel ferry

Anyone who peels the paint in the room or exhibits immoral pictures will be consigned to the authorities.

HOTEL ROOM NOTICE
Mexico City

NIGERIA HOTELS Ltd.

Kitchen Nursery 'A'

Economic Vegitarial & Stationery
Raw-Food Supplementary Up-Keep
Kitchen & Bar

To whom their duty som-times relied for the uses of our crops immediately don't forget before or after your off cut or harvesting any of the raw pastry *notice* the nursery gardner i/c whoes supplying records through i/c of the hotel manager are being treated.

BY ORDER

HOTEL NOTICE
Lagos

This, is today, a particular edition of a newspaper devoid of every form of entertainment or games, which tries to make your stay more cheerful, and in some cases more cultural even if in a small way, your holiday.

Considering every kind of stay in one country, we, by the simple language of this paper, tries to make your know of a big news, a very important initiative, that notable interest is going to gain in the whole of Europe. The Spring will see the inauguration here of a Centre for thermal treatments by the Thalasso-therapy.

The thalassotherapy in the actual society, where the indiscriminate use of medicines whatever is their employment, is bringing people to new kind of siknesses from medicaments, it assumes a consider-able importance just for its particularity due to the use, for the treatments, of the sea water.

Sea-water is mineral water of excellence, which contains 80% of the known chemical elements. For the thalassotherapy of these elements the salinity (the sea-water is classified as belonging to the salty iodie, bramine and sodium magnesian, clorurate type) the hydrostatic factor and thermality will be exploited.

The thalassotherapy and termal medicines, we have to recour to, more and more frequently, due, to the new-increasing occurence of work and street accidents, physichal strain and sedentarism due, to modern consumerism and the increase of sources of pollution.

The Centre has been progected according to the

more modern concepts, and it is adressed, not only for a curative purpose, but, at the more specifical end of prevention, therefore, the interested people, will not be only those of a certain age, present, only for a curative motive, but also, the young and the middle-aged people.

Big news will come from a 'Natural Therapy of Relax' and 'Silence treatment,' with the first therapy, will adopt 'Music-therapy' based on the exploitation of the catharsis activity of music, already known to the old greeks, the second will be practised in an ambit completly aphonic, with visualisation of natural backgrounds and projections of phantasmatical diapositives determing particular moods.

HOTEL INFORMATION SHEET
Crotone, Italy

In each room there is an apparatus placed to close the door, avoiding a dash. We kindly ask you by retracting yourself or leaving the room to check if the door is properly closed.

HOTEL ROOM NOTICE
Canary Islands

HYDRA – Intercourse means to the interior

Picture postcard caption
Hydra, Greece

PLEASE LEAVE YOUR DEPOSIT HERE.
THANK YOU.

Notice outside a
public convenience
Side, Turkey

SOME INSTRUCTIONS FOR THE WASHING

Plunge the shirt into not very hot water, taking care
no to compress her and not to twist her. Soap the
collar, the wristbands and the dirty parts and cleanse
washing out enough into luke warm water and after
into cold water.

Hang up the washed shirt (without squeezing her)
avoiding the formation of wrinkles especially in the
collar and wristbands; spread well the shirt on the
crutch buttoning her because she can retake her
natural position.

Expose the shirt for the drying and the shirt shall
be ready without ironing her. For a perfect pre-
servation of the freshness of the shirt repass now and
then the shirt with the smoothing iron.

Leaflet with a shirt
made in Italy

When meals are serviced in the Bedroom its price is increased with a 20% each dinner cause.

Please look the door.

Please close the fountains.

HOTEL ROOM NOTICE
Barcelona, Spain

BA BAIE WALE HOTEL

HAPPENISS CLEEN BATROWM
SHOWAR CHEP FAR TOREST

HOTEL ADVERTISEMENT
Kandahar, Afghanistan

**In rain contingency show will
take place in inside space**

NIGHT CLUB HANDBILL
Palamós, Spain

Violetta has absandonded a life of pleasure and vice to join Alfredo in a country toggace. Here her shameful past is washed away fore ver by a great passion.

OPERA HOUSE PROGRAMME
for *La Traviata*, Rome

100

THIS WATER IS PURIFIED AND GLORIFIED AND ABSOLUTELY SAFE FOR DRINKING

HOTEL ROOM NOTICE
Tehran, Iran

Clothes for street walkers

SHOP SIGN
Madrid

BUSINESSMEN!

Liable secretary available

HOTEL ROOM NOTICE
Helsinki, Finland

Suckling Pin
Lamp Spitted
Lambent Rails
Beef anc heep unixed
Lamb's Hers
Friend Pancakes

MENU ITEMS
Athens, Greece

Please see that lift is really
here before you open the door.

I will up
I will down

Enter the cabin of full lighting
only and never backwards.

Do not reverse into lift while lit up

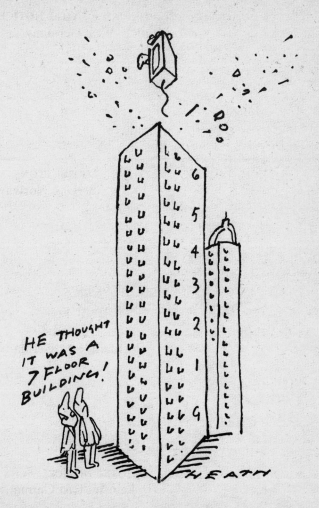

HE THOUGHT IT WAS A 7 FLOOR BUILDING!

GENERAL CONDITIONS

1 The vehicle will only be driven by the tenant and used for passengers-transportation, but is must never be used for goods transportation. Should the vehicle be apprehended because of the transportation of any fraudulent or stolen article or any object of uncertain origin, the whole responsability would the Client's.

2 The incidents which might happen against the complete accomplishment of this lease, will always be submitted to the juristiction of the Courts of Justice in Palma de Mallorca.

3 Moreover to what is foressen in the Law for the cases which are for themselves a transgression of the law, the Client driving a vehicle of the Firm under the influence of drugs, alcoholic drinks or having the mental powers disturbed by any other means, will assume the whole responsibility for the damages of the vehicle, and those caused to other vehicles, persons, objects, animals and to a 'third' in general.

The driver under the above mentioned circumstances will as well be responsibility for the persons and objects carged in the car.

4 The Client declares to have examined to his (her) content and satisfaction, the hired car and all its elements, including engine, steering-wheel body of the car and tyres. He (she) therefore declares that no responsibility whill concern the hiring-firm from any accident, incovenience, delay or difficulty whatsoever which might happen to him (her) or the other

car-travellers, not being among those convered by the all-risk-insurance which is granted by the hiring-Firm.

With full mutual agreement, both parties sing this lease on the above mentioned date.

CAR-HIRE CONTRACT
Majorca

PLEASE REPLACE UPROOTED SODS

GOLF COURSE NOTICE
Neuchâtel, Switzerland

The Museum is not responsible for damage or injury incurred by visitors through lack of care.

Please take care when descending stairways without railings, and avoid collision with showcases and windows.

MUSEUM TICKET
Jerusalem, Israel

Fried Milk

MENU ITEM
Marbella, Spain

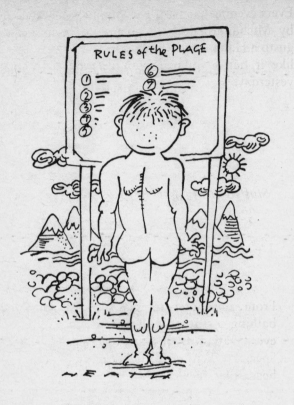

RULES OF THE PLAGE

Rule No. 6 Decency and good order will be maintained within the bounds of this establishment.

Rule No. 7 The bounds of this establishment reach only to this side of the rocks.

BATHING BEACH NOTICE
Lac Léman, Switzerland

Every evening you may listen to the concertos offered by Michail Kiriloff, playing with tenderness and gusto a Hammond-Combo Electric Organ. You will like it better today if you listened to it already yesterday.

HOTEL LEAFLET
Bucharest, Rumania

Stuffed meat copulate (fresh in the seasons)

MENU ITEM
Ankara, Turkey

From the hotel to sea directly with the bathing-costume. If you inform in adwance every variation of the menu has accepted. Special reduction for children and for many-headed families.

HOTEL NOTICE
Cattolica, Italy

We are No. 1 loafers, best in Bombay.

BAKERY SIGN
Bombay, India

Recently there have been frequent cases of un-apprehensive malinformed tourists of both sexes circulating through the streets in semi-nude veste-ments, exhibiting shamelessly their interiors and using very dishonest clothing which has caused livid protests from the public.

To avoid public scandal it has been advised to all owners of hotels and inns and to all persons that are obligated to call attention to these people who dress in such manner, to advise said people to circulate in public dressed honestly and to let them know that if they use these incorrect modes of dress that don't agreed with the moral customs of this country that they shall be severely punished by the competent authorities and that they also leave themselves open to the annoyance that the angry public might incur on them.

POLICE CIRCULAR
Granada, Spain

Please don't lay any stranger bodys in the WC

HOTEL NOTICE
Avallon, France

NO AUTOMOBILES. PEDERASTS ONLY.

Hotel courtyard sign
Barcelona, Spain

Sirs, Will you please control, before checking out, in the eventuality of your mistake, if do you change in own linen (bath towels, towels, etc.) endowing to the room, in which case, the staff is responsible of it.

Thanking you in advance for your attention, we give you a welcome, and have a very good stay.

The Management

HOTEL ROOM NOTICE
Naples, Italy

RESTAURANT WIENERWALD
At furnace: French chief of repute

A LA PATACHE
Gaspare – the boss at the cooker for
better you serve!

RESTAURANT 'LES CRUSTACES'
To take away: Lobster prepared or living

AEROGRILL
Ours chicken on the spit
Ours specialities
Ours menucard
In an unspoilable view: The Airport

For *your* advertising on the Belgian
Airports, apply to Air Terminal Publicity.

AIRPORT GUIDE
Brussels

MADRID

AT SAINT ISIDRO

Madrid, now, when this copy of TURISMO be in the street, will be living its days of Saint Isidro's feasts.

Madrid, at present, quite different from the Madrid of other epochs, is enjoying a lot of Spring days full of light, flowers and fair's climate.

Madrid, now, as ever, will be the capital that receives people from the four cardinal points of our geography that has the form of a bull's hide and from other hides beyond our frontiers.

Madrid, at present, quite different from how it was it is thirty years ago, keeps with its 'class' with its deepfelt traditions that the 'new times' and the 'new fashions' have not been able to efface.

Madrid, this Madrid of before, keeps living too, in spite of all the advancements and progress made within its arteries and its commercial lung very 'in' and actual.

At St. Isidro, the capital of the Kingdom is invaded by strangers that never feel so when they are here. These are the days of varied and lively feasts, of diverse events offered in a many coloured bouquet. Concerts, cultural events, full-fights, theatres, folklore exhibitions of the most genuine tradition, everything in an amalgam of events which have a true transcendence.

Madrid, the great city of the country, with its beautiful avenues, promenades and gardens, its monuments, its governmental buildings, its modern streets, its poetic places, its illumination, its traffic, its people, all this cause that the sojourn there during these days be for everybody a wonderful remembrance which is kept for ever in the file of our mind and we will never forget the hours and the days that we shall live here surrounded by the smoke and colour of St. Isidro's feats famous all over the world.

Madrid, the city of the bear and the madrono, always the capital of the nation, with peace and constant progress, opens the keyless doors and welcomes us with a true affection on these important dates in the annual calendar of its most dear feasts punctual to met everybody.

In tourism, Madrid, today as yesterday, and at all times, has a lot to offer us. It has always been so and it will be the same forever.

Madrid is worth of a travel from any place of the world.

This magazine sended among another agencies and offices in conexion with the tourism

From *Turismo* magazine
Madrid

Lamb shops
Reddening Meat
Speen omellet calf pluck
Buttrepishes
Salad of a Village
Bowels Tomato Special

MENU ITEMS
Crete

St. GEORGE HOTEL

Dear Passengers,
St. Georges Hotel Management is responsible for any inquiry and presents the following.

All services are to be required from the Management.

Please do not operate the Air Conditioner without advising the Hotel Management.

Please be tiny in not dropping your cigarette-tips out of the Ash-trays.

No woman is allow into your room except wife.
THANKS AND WELCOME
The Management

HOTEL NOTICE
Monrovia, Liberia

If you wish desinfection enacted on your presence, please ring for chambermaid.

HOTEL NOTICE
Lisbon

WITH THE HAIRDRESSER

If you are not more punctual in future, you will lose my custom.

Pray have the kindness to excuse me this time. I was sent for to a young bride, and it took me good while to invent a style of coiffure that set off her face.

Ah! you have put the brush into my mouth.

It was because you spoke when I did not expect it. The young bride's hair was blank, thick, coarse, her forehead broad and square. An ordinary hair-dresser would not have been able to hide the sternness of her features; but I have given her head a gentle and languishing expression.

Truly, I am struck with admiration. But, mister artist, with all your talent you have cut me; I am bleeding.

I have only taken off a little pimple. With a bit of court-plaster, it will not be seen.

From an English-Italian
conversation manual
published in Milan

Breast of Foul Chef
Farmercsstgle Omelet
Sloin Financier

MENU ITEMS
Valencia, Spain

Minner Water
Variety of Smoke
Strange Cheese

MENU ITEMS
Sofia, Bulgaria

Suggestive views from every window.

HOTEL BROCHURE
Amalfi, Italy

At the end to get always more agreeable and more recommending the stay in our hotels of Rome and Florence, we would be very grateful to our very appreciated clients and guests, if they want signalise us or by voice or by letter, any deficiency in the service, and also eventual advices which we would accept very willingly.

HOTEL ROOM NOTICE
Florence, Italy

The Beluga Restaurant, Marsascala Bay, will
be closed today due to the official opening.

Noodle of Bologna
Brood of Eels
Tart of This House

MENU ITEMS
Burgos, Spain

115

The books written on Corfu are so numerous, that one cannot know or cite them. Thus we shall only stop at the book of Laurence Durrell, *The Prosperous Cell*, which appeared in 1945. It is the diary of his stay in Corfu in 1937, inundated by a lyric torrent.

Kanoni is an incredible landscape, not because it is incredibly beautiful but because it is incredibly 'READY.' Imagination does not add nothing, you have nothing to do than to enclose it in frame.

NOTICE TO PASSENGERS

TOILETS

it is respectfully requesteb that Passengers refrain from throwing into the Pan any substance

LIKELY TO CHOKE THE PIPES

or prevent a proper flow of water, otherswise

SERIOUS DISCOMFORT TO PASSENGERS

themselves may be caused, and the toilet rendered both disagreeable and useless.
Passengers are earnestly desired to FLUSH the toilet before leaving.

PEOPLE ONLY

STREET SIGN
Jerusalem, Israel

All campers have to catch uq their waste water and to empty it on special places. in every case it is forbidden to empty it in the camp. It is strictly forbidden to use chemical WCs, because they constipate the outlets. Also it is forbidden to empty chemical water at the feet of trees.

CAMPSITE NOTICE
Southern France

SUD CARS offers a car in perfect condition check up.
Unlimited third party, our rates cover loss by theft, damages, fire, shuttering wind screen.
Delevery & Collection: Our cars can be delivered or recuperated at Railways stations, Airports, Ports and any Hotels.

CAR HIRE BROCHURE
Marrakech, Morocco

Real Pork

Label on pigskin handbag
Malaga, Spain

QUELUZ – A TOURISTIC EX-LIBRIS

by Manuel Martins

Nowadays tourism is a complexive form, including not only its first and elementary sense of travel-liking, but also a large concept connected to a structured organisation under the expression 'welcome' and giving to the foreigners who visit us, the most unforgettable remembrances.

For this, we must increase the plainness and courtesy of an affectionate people, knowing how to attract by the means of its natural sincerity, cementing the kind of tourism that spreads around the world – a tourism built by the mercantile concepts 'debit' and 'credit,' and turning it into a poetical and plain spirituality, that one can easily find among us.

Mother Nature gave us a large sum of attraction and the hand of men lent it an important collaboration.

We can easily look at Queluz, a touristic card of amazing coloured tints, turning themselves into a marvellous clima and a beautiful panormama, and all the delicate furniture of the Palace are a pleasure for the sight and an unforgettable remembrance forever.

TOURISM MAGAZINE
Lisbon

NO PERSON SHALL OBEY THE CALL
OF NATURE.
OFFENDERS WILL BE PROSECUTED.

> Building site
> notice, Hong Kong

This hotel is renowned for its peace and solitude. In fact, crowds from all over the world
flock here to enjoy its solitude.

> HOTEL BROCHURE
> Italy

OLD ENGLAND

ANTIQUES WITH EXPERTISES

from small acessory items to grandfathers

> BUSINESS CARD
> Mainz am Rhein, West Germany

He is formally forbidden so wash the cloth in
the bedrooms and to hang out him to
windows.

> HOTEL ROOM NOTICE
> Chambéry, France

LERICI – PORTOVENERE – CINQUE TERRE

Very pleasant full day excursion (or Half day) which leaving chaos, crowd and noisy Versilian street and beaches will bring you a serene rest thanks to the superb view offered by the magnificent gulf of La Spezia already immortalized by well know Poets among those one very sportly downed himself.

You wont regret to stroll along the side streets and lanes of Lerici or Portovenere, typical fishing villages where the sympathy and the rustic simplicity of the people make this picture indescriphable, living and picturesque.

The medieval castle dominating Lerici, forgotten sentinel against an enemi now vanished in the mist of centuries. is worse a visit even if 452 steps have to be climbed to reach the bastions.

Then, we carry on by boat along the very suggestive and incomparable Five Lands, villages forgotten by time and men very well known by their wine torn from the rocks after a very long and tiring work (*Water is for the rogues and the Deluge proved it – Noe*).

It is difficult to find true words to explain the courage and tenacity with which these men have dominated and conquered the adversity of the nature, keeping intact human values today vanished and which added to the wild surrounding nature, leaving a nostalgic souvenir.

TOURS BROCHURE
Viareggio, Italy

121

When you will call the reception, push on the red button, and leave the little button, on the left from the red button (on). If you don't will that the reception hear you, push the little button down (off). Attention: Don't push the red button when you speak.

HOTEL TELEPHONE LABEL
Brussels

You will feel like being at home.

HOTEL BROCHURE
Salzburg, Austria

DANGER

Forbidden by law to throw down stones or hardware. You could deadly injure people living or walking hereunder.

CLIFFTOP NOTICE
Capri

FOOT WEARING PROHIBITED

SIGN OUTSIDE SHRINE
Rangoon, Burma

The organistion of our Camping-Caravanning permit us to assure you all the confort suitable:

- Free and warm shower, bath, post sure, self-service, doctor, court for sports, etc.
- Piece of ground delimited, roosting of caravans, water, electricity, glide away.
- Prices of Prefecture, reduction for long stay and on reservation.
- Very good holidays in perspective without desa-greeable surprises.

CAMPING-SITE LEAFLET
Argelès-sur-Mer, France

MENU OF THE DAY

Mus be compuest of tho disher, bread and win, one of the disher has to be meat, chikoen or fisk includet bread & wine ¼L. or mineral water.

The composition of this menu is expesificate in separe paper.

RESTAURANT MENU
Malaga, Spain

Honor please with a visit our laces

POSTER
Positano, Italy

Nazaré is a privileged seaside resort where everything seems to be planned in order to seduce and attract visitors for a permanent and restful holiday-making.

Standing out from the whole scenery is the impressive belvedere of the Sitio Hill, the sight of which reaches the town and the endless sea.

It is here that the Miracle of Our Lady of Nazaré, dating back to the olden times of the Portuguese Nationality, had its origin.

According to tradition Dom Fuas Roupinho hunting on horseback when seanching a wild dear, was on the point of falling from the rock into the abyss below, but invoking the protection of Our Lady of Nazaré, was saved by a miracle.

> TOURIST OFFICE BROCHURE
> Portugal

Czardas Dish – specialities rich garnished, for 2 persons, served blazing

> MENU ITEM
> Gummersbach, West Germany

We would request our patrons not to leave taps open at night to avoid the disagreeable prospect of floods.

> HOTEL ROOM NOTICE
> Luand, Angola

Everyday vocabulary: *Food-poisoning, Forget it, Constipation, Strike-breaker, Easter, Pimp, Ostrich, Lack of show-off.*

John is studying the psychology of the pimp.
He spoke to me about his ostrich and the lack of show-off which ails him very often.

It is eighteen minutes past sixteen.
It is a quarter to fourteen.
It is fifteen minutes past twenty-two.

125

Who is the big-shot in this city? Is it that ridiculous
  knight-errant?
No. Nonetheless, he is the rubber-drive man. He
  knows about pill-boxes and sales-drive.
Who is that girl near your brother?

She is a glamour-girl. She has been in the jungle for
  ten years.
Are the other two fellows connections of hers?
No, one is a big-shot and the other is a cake-eater.
That flapper seems to be a gold-digger – am I
  right?
That is right. She left that poor boy embroiled.

Have you seen the medicine-man in the packing-
  house?

I would rather have a shorter life than be bald.

Have your friends good connections with those
  viscounts?
No, they have not. The viscounts are poor wretches,
  deviated beings of a consumed stupid generation.
  Those individuals have lost foot in the present.

Have you caught cold, or is it a defluxion?
Neither one. I am tired out.

Is your sister engaged?
Yes, she will be married soon.
Your cousin is chewing the cud.

How is your cousin this morning?
He is completely intoxicated.
Was your sister sick last year?
Yes, that was a case of food-poisoning. She had to
  be treated also of constipation.

Is this your mother-in-law's house?
Yes, it is true. It is as sure as death.

NEW BOOK SOON TO BE PUBLISHED: *How to Know and Exterminate Book Crackers.*

From *Teach Yourself English*,
published in Brazil

The hotel hall of exclusive price category offers peasant rest.

HOTEL ROOM NOTICE
Prague

PUBLIC ENTRANCE

NO ENTRY

Sign in
Maseru, Lesotho

Pork Loin with Jewess
Scrap-Heap Eggs
Various Slights

MENU ITEMS
Barcelona, Spain

Ladies and Gentlemen
Do You know where is situated the wonderful

INTERNATIONAL VILLAGGIO TURISTICO
RENAULT *GRANZOTTO*

of that all gone speak as the unique quiet watering-
place, with his Villas in a green etablishment.
This wonderful locality, the unique at the Adriatique
sea, with his blond sand, is situated in

BIBIONE (Venice)

Parents! For the sanity your children and for your
perfect recreation reserve a prety Villa in this quiet
oasis too You. After You come back every year!

129

Dear Friends

Famous doctors have been able to establish that the air and the sand of the coost Bibione, which contains a considerable percentage of iodine, brings the greatest therapeutic benefits in the months of May and September, and the rays of the sun in this season are the most advisable for the heliothrapeutic cure of children, as they radiate a mild warmth on them.

The pine forest of the Village whit the scene of resin and flowers, which are around the little villas offers to guests a relaxing stay and wonderful scenery in a true oasis peace. That said, and in consideration of the fact that in the aforementioned months You can obtain convenient prices, I am sure that avery father will be pleased to question me so that he can reserve a little villa in my Village.

These little villas are up to date and furnisched in a way to please the most demanding guests.

I take this occasion to send my best wishes to all friends of the *Villaggio Turistico* hoping that my wish will bring them good fortune, peace, and tranquility to Yours family. My partners join me in this, and I remind You that we are waiting to renew the hearty and affectionate welcome that my partners and I reserve for You to make You spend a joyful holiday as in the past.

Come in large numbers and come quickty!
Your cosy villa awaits you.
With sympathy and cordiality,
Yours sincerely
Amedeo Granzotto

REGULATIONS OF THE VILLAGE

1 Be welcome, Gentlemen and Ladies, at your home care of the *Villaggio Turistico*! If you will well treated, then tell it, please, to your friends and recommend to them our Village for their holidays.

2 The customers, who, because of whatever reason would fill hurt, or anyway not treated as it is their right, have to ask for it at once, as the owner himself or another person put at the head of the Management, always are present and at their complete disposal in order to be able to settle some possible dissensions.

3 All the claims that are not presented on the spot and in due time, can alter events from the realty. The season staff will not be present any more and it will not possible neither to ascertain the veracity of things nor to find out the right responsible one. As such claims when they are presented at a distance of time, then let think that they have a different purpose from that one of filling lawfully hurt, but only for another unavowable purpose. Being things so, all claims that are presented at a distance of time and not on the spot will not be taken into consideration.

4 The Management takes upon itself the care of putting to disposal the bungalows starting from the moment in which it receives the earnest or account, that has not to be lower than the 30% of the total amount of stay according to the price-list good for the year inst.

5 The customers, who, for some justified reasons, would not be able to enjoy their holidays, in order to have right to the reimbursement of what they have payed, that will be given back less the 10% for expenses, must pre-advise at least 15 days before their arrival; on the contrary, what was payed previously will be annexed and the bungalow will be at disposal for the days until the completion of the payed amount.

6 The Management is not responsible for things, jewels and values that would be lost or however stolen, as not delivered to the values-office of the Management itself, because a safe is at disposal of the customers for the free care as a guarantee of the above mentioned objects.

7 The Management begs the guests of its Village to close either doors or windows of the bungalow they live in and do not lay out any linen or anything else during the time they are absent, in order to avoid larency or theft.

8 The customers have not any right to occupy the bungalows before 12 o'clock of the day of their arrival and are requested to let them free before 10 o'clock on the day of their departure. That is worth in order to enable the proper staff of settling them in order.

9 The Management obliges their customers, at the moment in which they will take at delivery the bungalows awarded to them, to sign a copy of the whole furniture and fittings in them and they will be ansewerable for possible lacks or breakages.

10 The Management begs, besides, their customers, guests of the Village, to want to follow a good moral conduct, the laws that are regulating the seaside resorts and also all those rules regulating a good behaviour in common life, by observing the silence too ofter 22 o'clocks and avoiding, that is to say, troublesome noises that are able to disturb the night rest. Some possible recidivists will be considered as some displeasing persons and therefore invited to let the Village.

11 It is vorbidden to anyone to bring some beasts on the seashore and to let them take bath during the day-time; furthermore all the animals must be kept and enabled to not be hurtful and do not frighten the guests of the Village. Anyhow the owner of the beasts are responsible for them.

12 The Management of the Village does not take any care with regard to the use of gymnic-sporting fittings for children games, as these latter must taken care of by their parents; the same is worth in case of car accident within the Village itself, in which everyone must follow a speed not higher than 10 kilometers per hour, answerring personally for possible damages to persons or things of third persons.

13 The several Travel Offices are answerable for the customers they sent us for that which is concerning the due payment of stay, as we shall invoice it to themselves; while, vice-versa, we shall cash directly from the customers the extras only; remaining unchanged for the Travel Offices

too either the contents of the paragraphs Nr. 4 and 5 or the observance of the whole Regulation of the *Villaggio Turistico*.

HOLIDAY VILLAGE BROCHURE
Bibione, Italy

Hot and cold water running up and down the stairs.

HOTEL NOTICE
Sweden

All minuet steaks are boiled in charl coal

MENU NOTE
Corfu

For everybody's convenience it is not allowed to come into the building with the feet full with sand.

HOTEL NOTICE
Costa Brava, Spain

Coffins to sell at opportunity prices

CEMETERY SIGN
Famagusta, Cyprus

We have nice bath and are very good in bed.

HOTEL BROCHURE
Zurich, Switzerland

Friend Cod
Assaulted Artichoke
Eggs Good Woman
Rape, Seamanlike Style

MENU ITEMS
Seville, Spain